EL PASO'S
GEOLOGIC
PAST

EL PASO'S GEOLOGIC PAST

by Earl M. P. Lovejoy
Revisions by William C. Cornell

Texas Western Press
The University of Texas at El Paso
1996

Second Edition, revised 1996
First Edition, 1980
Library of Congress Catalog No. 96-60101
ISBN 0-87404-065-5

Cover photo by C.D. Walcott, The Franklin Mountains, 1896.
(Courtesy: U.S. Geological Survey)

∞ Texas Western Press books are printed on acid-free paper,
meeting the guidelines for permanence and durability of the
Committee on Production Guidelines for Book Longevity of the
Council on Library Resources.

CONTENTS

Preface to the Second Edition

Since 1980, when *El Paso's Geologic Past* first appeared, this book has been popular with El Pasoans interested in the unusually rich geologic setting of their community. Professor Lovejoy became an El Pasoan in 1965, when he joined the geology faculty of Texas Western College (now the University of Texas at El Paso). His earlier career had included stints as a hard rock miner, an engineering geologist, an exploration geologist for the Atomic Energy Commission, and as a mines claims examiner for the Bureau of Land Management. His geologic interests extended from the Big Bend country through El Paso outward across the Basin and Range and Colorado Plateau regions of the American southwest. El Paso, however, was special.

He recognized the diversity of the geologic features of the area and took advantage of them in all his teaching activity. His favorite "classroom" was an outcrop for he firmly believed that geology is best comprehended by looking at the rocks, their structures, even their fossils. "Put your hand on it" was an oft heard phrase when one was in the field with him. In *El Paso's Geologic Past*, Earl intended that each reader should be able to find and to put his hand on rocks or other features critical to understanding that past, and to appreciate something of their significance.

In geology, as in other sciences, ideas are proposed, tested, fine-tuned, sometimes refuted and discarded. Some of our ideas about El Paso's geology are different than they were in 1980. In up-dating the text, I have tried to maintain Earl's writing style while incorporating these revised ideas. One entirely new section, on the Rio Grande Rift, has been added. In 1980, few geologists knew much about the Rio Grande Rift or about continental rifts like it worldwide. Today, we realize that the Rio Grande Rift is one of a handful of "failed" continental rifts and is, potentially, crucial to understanding rifting in the larger process of global tectonics. Other changes include up-dating the publications list for those readers seeking more detailed information. Terrie Cornell assisted in up-dating the road log for the self-guided field trip.

William C. Cornell
March 1996

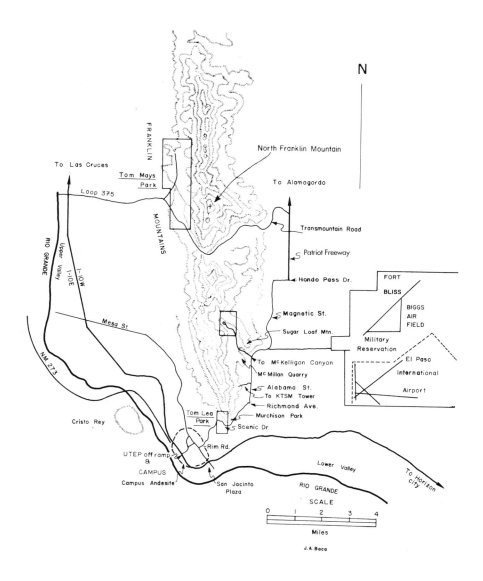

N

Fig. 1. Local index map of El Paso and vicinity.

The Rio Grande

Although the towering Franklin Mountains are the most obvious geologic feature of the El Paso region (Fig. 1), the Rio Grande Valley remains the most important feature to the citizens of El Paso County. The early settlers used the river water and the rich flood plain soils for agriculture and ranching. Modern downtown El Paso and Ciudad Juárez rest primarily on the flood plain of the river, and the rich farm-lands of the upper and lower valleys are based on the alluvial soil derived from the flood waters of the river.

To El Pasoans of the nineteenth century, the recurring annual cata-strophic floods of the Rio Grande were a threat which demanded a solution — an upstream dam, begun in 1911 at Elephant Butte, New Mexico (Fig. 2). During most of the year, the river was a gentle source of life and sustenance, its placid waters unique in this harsh Chihuahuan desert, its flat flood plain a fertile valley in which gener-ous vineyards flourished and cattle grazed on rich stands of lush grass. But during the spring, the river's normal trickle swelled to a torrent which raged for weeks, spreading rampaging flood waters far north into what is now San Jacinto Plaza, the heart of downtown El Paso, separating the settlements on each side of the river by a wide stretch of impassable flood, destroying man's works, carrying huge volumes of silt and unused water to the sea, and changing its course from one part of the valley to another. As the last of the winter's snows melted from the high peaks of the San Juan and Sangre de Cristo mountains of New Mexico and Colorado and the spring flood ebbed, vast sheets of newly deposited mud, silt, and sand remained on the flood plain, spread from bank to bank. This annual replenishment of the fertile river alluvium formed a base on which the verdant growth of the val-ley flourished through the long, hot summers. Fresh, sweet water which lay just below the surface of the flood plain was raised from shallow dug wells and supplied the needs of the populace. Because water which flowed unused to the sea was wasted, El Pasoans in 1904 recommended the construction of a dam at Elephant Butte to impound the unused water for irrigation as well as to stop the floods. By 1916, the dam was completed and flood waters no longer freely flowed to the sea.

But the Rio Grande had not always freely flowed to the sea. Millions of years ago, it ended near El Paso; its sediments filled in the great basins of this region and a broad, ephemeral lake, called Lake Cabeza de Vaca, spread widely in the valleys between the Hueco

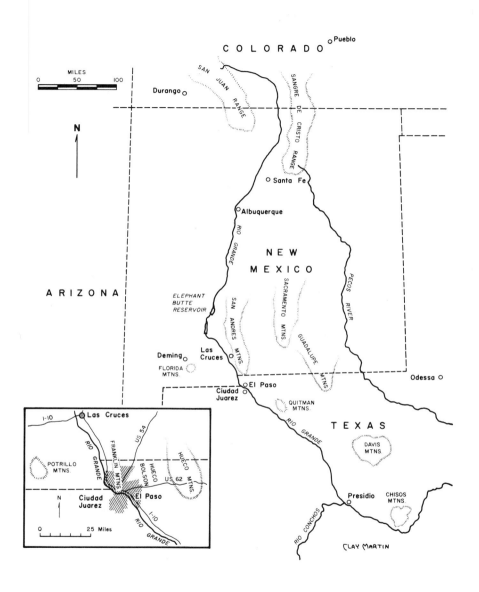

Fig. 2. Regional index map of the Rio Grande.

Mountains to the east and the Potrillo Mountains to the west. For millions of years the ancestral Rio Grande poured flood waters and river alluvium (or sediment) into this region and, as the basins filled with sediment, the lake spread out into a broad, shallow sheet of water which in dry seasons would completely evaporate, leaving only a broad flat valley floor. During rainier times, the lake spread and deepened. The lake probably flowed over the rim south of the Quitman Mountains, and the outflow joined the much larger Rio Conchos from Mexico, finally flowing to the sea.

Although the lake is gone, its sediments remain as do those of the ancient river (Fig. 3). These river and lake sediments fill the basins to great depths; as much as 9,000 feet of them underlie Fort Bliss.

The ancient river and lake deposits (called the Fort Hancock Formation) are the sedimentary formations on either side of the Rio Grande's upper and lower valleys. They are exposed widely below Rim Road and along Mesa, Magnetic, and Alabama streets as well as Interstate 10 west of downtown El Paso and NM 273 west of the Upper Valley north of Sunland Park, New Mexico. They underlie Fort Bliss, Biggs Field, El Paso International Airport, and the broad flat plains east of the Franklin Mountains (the Hueco bolson) and west of the upper valley (La Mesa).

The Franklin and Hueco mountains, Sierra de Juárez, and the upper part of Cerro de Cristo Rey all projected above the flood plain of the ancestral Rio Grande. When Lake Cabeza de Vaca overflowed near the Quitman Mountains, the river started to cut down into the poorly consolidated horizontal river and lake sediments and the present valley of the Rio Grande began. This part of the river formed its present valley about one million years ago. Earlier, while the river was still filling the basins, it once flowed along the east side of the Franklin Mountains. Deposits of river sands almost 1,500 feet thick just beneath the surface are filled with fresh ground water; El Paso gets much of its city water from these old river deposits.

Fig. 3. This outcrop of the Fort Hancock Formation is on the west side of I-10 at the top of the hill between Executive Center and Sunland Park exits.

Fig. 4. This kind of volcano is called a cinder cone because it is composed of volcanic rock fragments of sand-to-gravel size called cinders or ash. Cinder cones may vary from 1,000 feet to over a mile wide at the base and can be hundreds to a few thousand feet high. They may occur in groups or clusters as volcanic fields. Most cinder cones are made of a black, dense rock called basalt. The cinder cone is steep because the cinders have accumulated by falling from the eruption cloud and now lie at the angle of repose; they cannot form a steeper slope because they will roll down the side if it is any steeper. Most cinder cones erupt and die in a few years or a few decades and become extinct, never to erupt again.

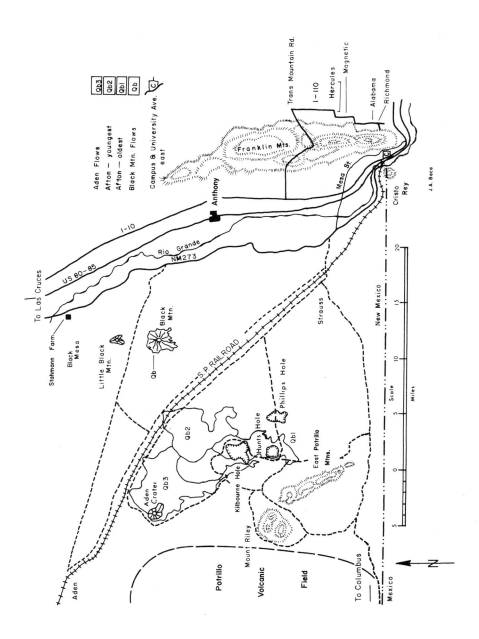

Fig. 5. Index map of Potrillo Mountains region.

6

Volcanoes

As the Rio Grande was deeply cutting its present valley several hundred thousand years ago, twenty miles to the west of the valley great eruptions of molten lava and volcanic cinders and ash produced extensive lava deposits and about one hundred cinder cone volcanoes (Fig. 4) on top of the old river sediments of the La Mesa plains (Fig. 5). This volcanic field is now known as the Potrillo Mountains. Black lava rose along fractures or faults in the crust of the earth (Fig. 6), rising from depths as much as fifty miles, at temperatures of about 2,000°F. As the lava met the ground water in the old river sediments, it explosively changed the water to steam, and lava exploded into fine ash and cinders. Lava, steam, ash, and cinders emerged onto the surface, usually early in violent eruptions (Fig. 7), generally later as quiet flows (Fig. 8). Incandescent lava, bright red to yellowish white in night-time darkness, flowed downhill from the volcanoes, merging as sheets of slowly moving, dense liquid, engulfing trees, filling depressions, and forming a type of igneous (derived from molten rock-forming materials called lava or magma) rock named basalt.

Eruptions in the Potrillo volcanic field continued for thousands of years, first one volcano, then another. Some of the final volcanoes formed in the upper valley near the present Stahmann Farms. The basalt lava flowed down to the river level about 40,000 years ago. Since that time, the river has eroded seventy feet, and the old basalt flow now stands as a black mesa about seventy feet above the present river flood plain (Fig. 9).

In several places, the lava produced so much explosive steam as it boiled the ground water that great volumes of the old river sediment were blown out around the vent; little volcanic cinder or ash accumulated, and only a small amount of lava emerged. These violent steam eruptions excavated broad, funnel-shaped holes about one mile wide in the readily erodible river sediments. Much of the airborne debris fell back into the funnels (Fig. 10), partially refilling them. Other debris fell around the funnel margins building up rims, thicker on the downwind side. Undoubtedly, some of the finer-grained dust and ash was widely distributed over the adjacent countryside. During the millennia since the eruptions, erosion of the walls of the funnels has filled them still more. Today the holes are a few hundred feet deep and the rims are low, rounded ridges twenty to fifty feet high (Fig. 11). Several of these holes, or maars (pronounced "mars"), lie east of the Potrillo volcanic field. Their names — Hunt's Hole, Kilbourne Hole,

Phillips' Hole — commemorate early ranchers in the region.

Today the violent eruptions are gone; the thunderous steam explosions are silent; the brilliant scarlet glare reflected from the low, overhanging cinder-laden eruption clouds has faded into the brilliant hues of thousands of desert sunsets; only the stark, barren, pitch-black basalt rock of the lava flows and cinder cones remains to remind us of the volcanic pyrotechnic displays of many millennia ago.

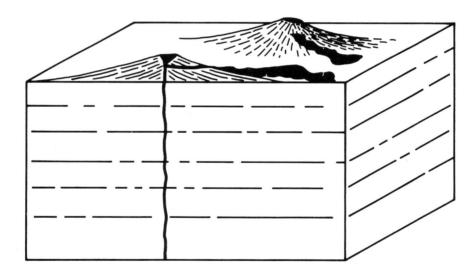

Fig. 6. Dikes are intrusions into older rock as volcanoes occur. White-hot lava which forms volcanoes comes up from depths of as much as fifty miles along fractures or faults in the crust of the earth. The lava (or magma, as it is called before it reaches the surface) rises so rapidly that it does not have time to cool so that it emerges on the surface at about the temperature it had at depth. If the lava reacts with water in the ground, it produces great steam explosions. The lava is then broken into small pieces which are thrown out onto the surface as ash. Late in the eruption, lava usually emerges from the flanks of the volcano.

Fig. 7. A cinder cone is seen here in eruption. White-hot lava has con-
tacted the ground water and produced great billows of white steam
which rise tens of thousands of feet in the air, extending downwind
for hundreds of miles. Entrapped in the boiling steam cloud are vast
quantities of ash, carried to great heights in the turbulent steam. The
coarser ash falls out quickly near the vent, forming the cinder cone.
Finer material is carried leeward, laying down a carpet of volcanic tuff
downwind from the cone. For example, in the year 79 Pompeii was
buried by such an eruption of tuff from Mount Vesuvius. This phase
of volcanic formation may last intermittently for years.

Fig. 8. Lava may flow from cinder cones. As the last phase of cinder cone eruption, the basalt lava may rise high in the cone and form a pool. Generally, the volcano is not strong enough to support such a large pool of dense lava and the crater or the side of the cone breaks. Sometimes the lava emerges from the central dike as well. The lava flows out the side of the volcano as a flank eruption. The lava is intensely hot and continues as a liquid for hours and days so that it can flow great distances from the volcano. Here two volcanic eruptions have occurred simultaneously and the lava flows are shown to have merged downstream where they are spreading out on a broad plain.

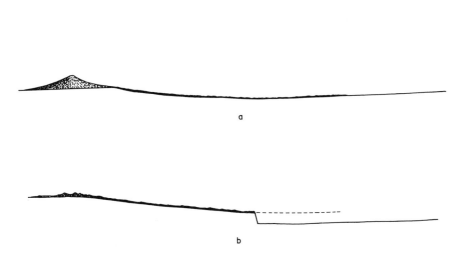

a

b

Fig. 9. The sequence of geologic events at Stahmann Farms started (a) with the eruption of a small cinder cone. A flank eruption of basalt lava emerged and flowed eastward onto the flood plain of the Rio Grande about 40,000 years ago during the last of the major Pleistocene ice ages. During voluminous outflow of glacial melt water down the Rio Grande (b), the river valley was deepened seventy feet by erosion, leaving the lava flow that far above the present river valley. The cinder cone has been greatly modified by erosion by rain.

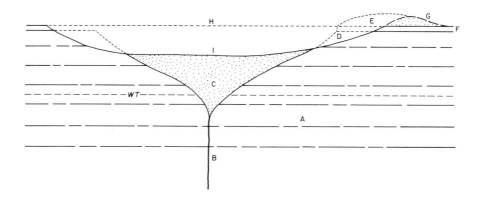

Fig. 10. This cross section of a typical maar shows (A) the stratified deposits through which the dike (B) has penetrated to form the maar. The maar is filled with churned and reworked (A) material (C) which is mixed with eroded material (D) from the rim-rock (E). Material ejected from the maar during eruption forms a lip (G) around the maar. The original extent of the surface of the stratified deposits is shown as (H). As the magma in the dike (B) reacted with water below the water table (WT), great volumes of steam formed which produced the violent eruptive activity of maar formation. Maars probably form when there is much ground water and less lava; volcanoes probably form when there is less ground water and more lava.

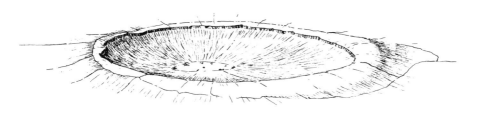

Fig. 11. This idealized sketch view of a maar shows a dry lake in the bottom in which a small building has been erected. A road extends around the rim-rock edge of the maar.

The Seas

To believe that the great seas at one time swept over this vast region must test the credulity of today's discerning observer. The roar of stormy sea surf crashing against rocky promontories or the quiet lapping of the gentle wavelets on a sandy beach are sounds now absent in our desert; the seas are hundreds of miles away, thousands of feet lower. One hundred million years ago, marine waters inundated as much as half of North America; shallow salt water spread as far west as Las Vegas, Nevada, and as far east as Minnesota and from the Gulf of Mexico to the Arctic Sea. The low borderlands loomed darkly forested to the east and west. Dinosaurs roamed the tidelands and plains, plesiosaurs swam the seas, and pterodactyls floated ponderously in the tropic air. No bird calls echoed at eventide; mammals were but tiny occupants of a land of giants; of the intellect of man there was no clue.

Continental lands rise and fall, slowly, almost imperceptibly in the life span of man, but the crust of the earth rises and falls thousands of feet over millions of years. Sea level changes imperceptibly as well, depending on the amount of polar glacial ice which holds sea water in reserve and according to the form and volume of the ocean basins. Changes in elevation of the land and the sea produce advances and retreats of shorelines. This combination also causes flooding of the continental interiors, during which time the sediments we now see in the mountains were deposited.

Just as the Rio Grande deposited vast sheets of alluvium in the basins around El Paso a few million years ago, so have ancient rivers carried river sediment into the sea (much as the Mississippi River has carried silt into the Gulf of Mexico) throughout geologic time (Table 1). The coarse material from the rivers is deposited near shore; finer sand forms the beaches and offshore sand bars. Still finer material is deposited farther from shore, carried out to sea by wave and current motions, and forms muds in the slightly deeper waters. Farther out at sea, beyond the point where all the sediment has settled out, the water is clear and little terrestrial sediment accumulates (Fig. 12).

Sediment in the sea can accumulate in great thickness. Although the sand along the beach may be thick a few tens of feet, deposits may, over long periods of time, accumulate to hundreds and thousands of feet thick (Fig. 13). Mud and sand at the mouth of the Mississippi River have accumulated in the Gulf of Mexico to a thickness of 40,000 feet in the past twenty-five million years. This thickness is much greater than the average; usually, marine deposits on the surface of the earth are not so great; thicknesses of thousands of feet are more usual.

The interesting point about the sediments in these great accumulations is that they all formed in shallow water only a few hundred feet deep. How can thousands of feet of sediment accumulate in water only a few hundred feet deep? The evidence indicates that locally the ocean bottom gradually sinks in a broad basin and the sediment accumulates in that basin. This type of local sinking of the ocean bottom to produce basins occurs all over the world; therefore, the continents rise broadly over vast areas; sea level rises and falls; the sea floor locally moves up and down, relatively rapidly in terms of geologic time, thereby producing sedimentary basins in which sediments accumulate in greater than normal thicknesses. The present Gulf of Mexico is one such sedimentary basin. The Permian Basin of West Texas is a similarly formed seafloor basin in which huge volumes of oil formed and accumulated. Many major oil producing regions of the world occur in such marine basins.

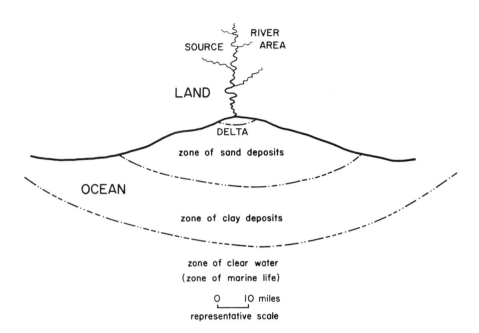

Fig. 12. Distribution of different types of marine sediments is shown offshore from the source area. Erosion by running stream waters from the source area on land produces gravel, sand, and clay particles which are carried down the river and into the sea. Wave action separates the coarser and finer materials, carrying the finest particles, clay, far out to sea, and leaving the coarser sand and gravel deposited near shore. Sand (not shown) is carried all along the shore as beach sands and offshore bars for great distances, but these deposits are within a short distance of the shoreline. In the deeper and clearer water marine organisms abound and their skeletons form limestones. This is a generalized concept; numerous exceptions occur.

Fossils

One of the common types of inquiries received by the paleontologists (geologists who study fossils) in the El Paso Geological Society concerns the sea shells which rock hounds, students, and hikers find in the Franklin Mountains. That they are sea shells is obvious to these amateur collectors, but what is not so obvious is how they got there.

Fossils (Fig. 14) are defined by paleontologists as evidence of prehistoric life. Bones of wooly mammoths, shells from mollusks, footprints of dinosaurs, all of these are fossils. Although life has existed on earth for at least 3.5 billion years, evidence of former life is not always preserved. Scavengers eat the flesh; weathering destroys the bones and shell material; erosion carries away the debris. Fossils are remarkable for no other reason than that something was preserved. So abundant has been past life that the preservation of even 1 percent of the total has given rise to vast accumulations of fossil material. Given the abundance of fossils, imagine the abundance of ancient life!

Modern seas abound with animals such as corals, clams, shrimp, lobsters, and sharks. Some, like the corals, are "rock builders." Corals secrete great volumes of calcium carbonate and build massive reefs like those that form the Bermuda and Bahama islands and the Great Barrier Reef east of Australia. Others, like the clams, live solitary lives, embedded in clay muds near shore. Still others move about on the bottom of the sea, scavenging from the multitudes on the sea floor. Predators like the lobster attack the bottom-dwelling animals. Above all ominously glide the silent sharks, the tigers of their realm living on the fish of the sea.

Shells of most marine animals are made of a substance abundant as dissolved material in sea water, calcium carbonate. In its solid form, calcium carbonate is a mineral called calcite. Pearl and marble both are forms of calcite. The shells of coral are calcite, and as a result, the great reefs produced by the corals and the other sea animals and plants that live with them are formed of calcite. Seafloor scavengers devour sea animals, shells and all, and grind up the shells into small fragments which are then deposited on the sea floor as calcareous (derived from calcite) muds and sands. Thus, the sea floor in regions of clear water far offshore in the places where marine life abounds consists of calcareous sands and muds, reefs, dead bodies of various types of sea animals, and plants. When these huge accumulations of calcite are raised above sea level (as they are in the Franklin Mountains), they form limestone rock.

In general, sea life prefers to live in clear water, beyond the zone where the coastal sand and clay accumulate (Fig. 12). But some types do not mind the murky coastal waters and therefore fossils can be found even in sand and clay deposits. Sometimes sea plants are of more local importance than are sea animals. Seaweed, sea ferns, kelp, and algae are abundant in certain parts of the ocean. Without the plants and algae, the animals would have nothing on which to feed, the food chain would not have a beginning, and sea life could not exist. Many of the algae are also producers of calcite. Much of the limestone in the Franklin Mountains contains abundant fossil algae, including the oldest fossils in the region, about one billion years old.

In the Franklin Mountains, in the Sierra de Juárez, and around Cerro de Cristo Rey, large accumulations of fossil material exist. The careful observer notes that certain fossil types occur only in certain rock units. For example, a type of mollusk called *Gryphaea* found in a limestone around Cerro de Cristo Rey is not found in the older rocks of the Franklin Mountains. This relationship between the fossils and the rocks in which they occur indicates to paleontologists the geologic age of the formation in which the fossils are found.

Fossils found in one sequence of sedimentary rocks over a wide area are called index fossils; index fossils are remains of animals or plants that lived over a wide area (such as all the Atlantic Ocean) for a geologically short time (perhaps a few hundred thousand years). Using index fossils, paleontologists can determine the geologic age of formations, thereby relating all formations with the same or closely related index fossils all over the world to the same geologic time. For example, an extinct crablike sea animal called a trilobite existed world-wide in Cambrian time, was much less abundant in Silurian time, and became extinct at the end of the Permian (see Table 1). Thus, a limestone containing abundant trilobites could not be younger than Permian and would probably be Cambrian. By knowing the exact geologic age range of thousands of different types of index fossils, paleontologists can determine the precise geologic period or age of any rocks which contain these fossils.

Fig. 13. These rugged peaks north of Woodrow Bean Transmountain Drive on the east side of the Franklin Mountains are formed on Precambrian Lanoria Quartzite. Originally horizontal, these sedimentary rocks now are inclined or dip toward the west about 35° as the result of tilting of the Franklin Mountains. The sands which form the rocks were deposited near the seashore about one billion years ago.

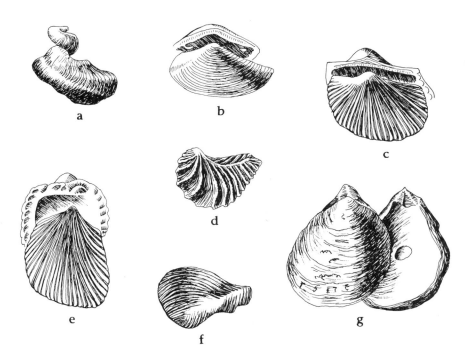

Fig. 14. These bivalve mollusks lived in the warm shallows of the Cretaceous sea which covered the El Paso region 120 million years ago. They are: (a) *Exogyra*, one to two inches; (b) *Nuculana*, one to two inches; (c) *Cucullaea*, one to two inches; (d) *Trigonia*, one to two inches; (e) *Cardium*, one to two inches; (f) *Corbula*, 0.5 inch; and (g) *Ostrea*, five to six inches. *Exogyra* is extinct but living relatives of all the others can be found on seashores in various parts of North America today. These fossils can be found in the sedimentary rocks near Mount Cristo Rey. They are most abundant in the shales but may be found in the limestones as well. The Muleros Formation is largely a *Gryphaea* bank, like a modern oyster reef.

Rocks

In the solar system the outer planets — Jupiter, Saturn, Uranus, Neptune, and Pluto — are formed of materials like carbon dioxide (the bubbly gas in soft drinks and beer) which are normally gases on Earth; on those planets the temperatures are so low that these substances are reduced to the solid state, much like commercial dry ice is the solid state of carbon dioxide. The Sun is a white hot, incandescent gas. Only the inner planets (Mercury, Venus, Earth, and Mars) are made of rock. Thus, what we call rock on Earth represents only a small proportion of the material of the solar system.

The rock on Moon, Mars, Venus, and Mercury is similar to the common volcanic rock on Earth, basalt. No evidence indicates that there ever was an ocean system on the Moon, Venus, Mercury, or Mars, although some evidence suggests that there might have been rivers on Mars. Thus, Earth is the only planet on which widespread planetary pools of water exist.

Rocks formed from molten material like lava or magma are called igneous rocks. Rocks formed from sediments deposited in bodies of water are called sedimentary rocks. Because of the erosion of land and the deposition of sediments in the world-wide oceans on Earth, there is also widespread distribution of sedimentary rocks. About three-fourths of the surface of Earth is covered by marine sedimentary rocks. Marine sediments are usually deposited essentially flat on the bottom of the sea. These originally horizontal layers of sediment are called strata or beds. The banding visible on the east side of the Franklin Mountains is bedding of sedimentary rocks.

The three principal types of sediments deposited in the sea are (1) sand, (2) clay, and (3) calcareous materials derived from plants and animals. Sand becomes cemented by various types of cement to form sandstone; if the cement is silica (which is very strong), the sandstone is called quartzite. Clay becomes compacted by the weight of overlying sediment to form a sedimentary rock called shale. Calcareous sediments become limestone as the result of a process called recrystallization.

Geologists give proper names to rocks to make their descriptions easier. For example, the sedimentary rocks in the Franklin Mountains were first named by a United States Geological Survey geologist, G. B. Richardson, in 1909; he referred to some of them in the southern Franklin Mountains as the Bliss Sandstone, the El Paso Limestone, and the Montoya Dolomite (dolomite is a variety of calcite). The term formation may also be used in place of the rock type, as in the Bliss Formation. These sedimentary rocks have index fossils similar to those found in southwestern England where Ordovician strata were named, the so-called type locality of Ordovician strata. Therefore, Richardson knew that these rocks in the Franklin Mountains were also of Ordovician age. A sedimentary rock can be designated, therefore, in three ways: first, by the rock type (for example, limestone); second, by its proper name (for example, the El Paso Limestone); and third, by its age (for example, Ordovician). The full description would then be: Ordovician El Paso Limestone.

Almost all of the sedimentary rocks of the El Paso region have been named, described, and dated (Tables 2 and 3). Not all of them are readily visible from highways or distinguishable from one another to the untrained eye, but some of the more widely exposed and easily identified strata in the southern Franklin Mountains include the El Paso Limestone (Figs. 15 and 16) and the Montoya Dolomite of Ordovician age and the Fusselman Limestone of Silurian age.

For example, Scenic Drive Park lies on the contact (that is, the surface where one sedimentary rock unit lies on top of another) between the Florida Mountains Formation of the El Paso Limestone and the darker gray Upham Formation of the Montoya Dolomite (Fig. 15). Most of Scenic Drive east of the park has been excavated in the El Paso Limestone, but most of the drive west of the park is in Montoya Dolomite. The TV towers on the ridge north of Scenic Drive Park (Fig. 16) are built on the Montoya Dolomite which forms the ridge of the range. Farther north, KTSM-TV tower is on the Scenic Drive Formation in the upper part of the El Paso Limestone. Most of the west side of the southern Franklin Mountains (south of South Franklin Mountain) is formed on the Montoya Dolomite (Fig. 17). The Sierra de Juárez is formed of Cretaceous limestone; the various formations are not readily distinguishable when viewed from downtown El Paso. Although all of them have been named, the names will not be given here. The Cretaceous formations around Cerro de Cristo Rey have also been named by geologists, but they are not easily identifiable from a distance and therefore their names will not be given here.

Fig. 15. These marine strata are exposed on the northern side of Scenic Drive at the south end of the Franklin Mountains at Scenic Drive Park. Originally deposited horizontally, they dip west as the result of the tilting of the Franklin Mountains. These deposits were formed in shallow, warm seas by numerous plants and marine animals. The blocky beds on the right and the thin-bedded strata in the center are part of the Florida Mountains Formation, a distinctive buff unit of the southern Franklin Mountains. The massive, blocky strata on the left are part of the Upham Formation which forms the ridge line of the southern Franklin Mountains near Scenic Drive.

Fig. 16. These west-dipping beds form the ridge north of Scenic Drive at the south end of the Franklin Mountains at Scenic Drive Park. The ridge-forming, massive, blocky bed is the Upham Formation of the Ordovician Montoya Dolomite. The strata to the right are part of the Scenic Drive Formation of the Ordovician El Paso Limestone. The Florida Mountains Formation is partly obscured by an accumulation of rock fragments at the bottom of the Upham Formation.

Fig. 17. These high, rugged peaks of Mount Franklin (elevation 6,186 feet), viewed from the west, are formed on the light-colored Cutter Formation. The slightly darker strata which form most of the slope are of the Upham and Aleman Formations. The strata dip toward the observer, or toward the west.

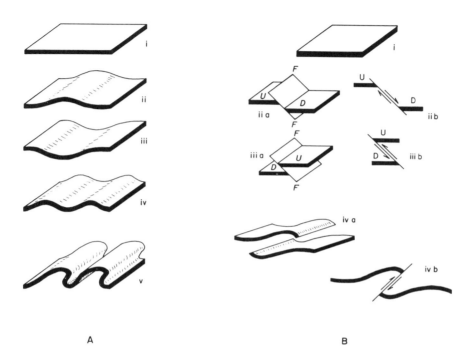

Fig. 18. Folded (A) and faulted (B) strata are illustrated here. A horizontal stratum (A-i) is folded into a type of fold called an anticline (A-ii) or a syncline (A-iii). Gently folded strata form two anticlines and a syncline (A-iv). Severely folded strata have been deformed into two anticlines and a syncline (A-v). A horizontal stratum (B-i) has been faulted (B-iia) with one side of the fault moving relatively upward (B-U), the other side relatively downward (B-D). A cross section (B-iib) shows the sense of movement by arrows; the fault in this case is a normal fault. The fault illustrated in B-iiia and B-iiib is a reverse fault. The stratum in B-iva has been folded and faulted by a low angle reverse, or thrust, fault, as shown in the cross section (B-ivb).

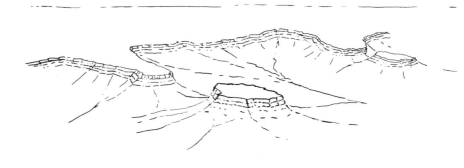

Fig. 19. Mountains formed by erosion are illustrated by flat lying strata that have been eroded by streams leaving erosional remnants as isolated mountains or hills. Erosion will eventually destroy the outlying hills and will erode all the strata completely.

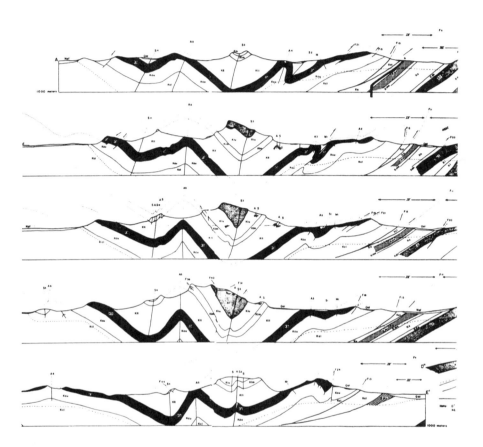

Fig. 20. Cross sections of Sierra de Juárez by Herbert Wacker show an interpretation of the structure. The right side of the diagram is toward the northeast, the left side toward the southwest. The black unit represents the Cretaceous Benigno Formation; the shaded unit represents the Finlay Formation. Between those two is the Lágrima Formation, and beneath the Benigno Formation is the Cuchillo Formation. Both the Lágrima and the Cuchillo formations contain subdivisions or members that are shown.

Mountains

Of all the geographical features on the surface of Earth, perhaps the most awesome are mountains. Geologists have classified mountains primarily by the processes which produced them. Among them are volcanic mountains such as Mount Rainer, the product of great eruptions during millions of years. Examples of small volcanic mountains are the cinder cones of the Potrillo volcanic field, each of which was produced probably in only a few years. Some mountains are produced by deep erosion processes, lasting millions of years, of highly uplifted parts of earth's crust (such as Mount Everest which contains marine sedimentary rocks over five miles above sea level). Some mountains are the result of severe deformation of originally horizontal sedimentary rocks; this deformation, which may take tens of millions of years to occur, may consist of two different types: folding and faulting. Superficially, folded strata resemble folded rugs, pushed along the floor and crumpled against the wall, sometimes only slightly rumpled, sometimes thoroughly contorted (Fig. 18A). Faulted strata resemble broken blocks of concrete; the faults are fractures in the crust of the Earth where the rocks on each side have moved along the fracture distances varying from inches to miles (Fig. 18B). Some other mountains are formed rather quickly, it is believed, by emplacement of magma into strata near the surface of the Earth; the magma may bulge the overlying strata upward like a big blister (Fig. 23).

Erosion is important in the formation of all mountains. While a mountain is being formed, rainfall tends to erode it; a constant battle is waged between the constructional processes trying to build the mountain and the erosional processes trying to tear it down. When the building processes are faster, the mountain grows; when the eroding processes are faster, the mountain shrinks.

Near El Paso are hills and mountains formed by all of these various processes. The cinder cone volcanoes of the Potrillo volcanic field have already been described. The Rio Grande is eroding into the ancient river deposits of the Fort Hancock Formation, forming a valley; the edges of the valley will look more like hills as the valley progressively deepens and the topography becomes more rugged (Fig. 19). The strata in the Sierra de Juárez, once horizontal, have been intensely folded. Although most of the folds are not readily apparent from El Paso, geological mapping of the range has shown their existence with great precision and accuracy (Fig. 20). One fold in the range is readily visible from southwestern El Paso. The strata in the

Franklin Mountains, once horizontal, have been faulted, raised thousands of feet, and tilted toward the west in the process of faulting (Fig. 21). Cerro de Cristo Rey (Fig. 22) contains a central core of igneous rock, formed when magma intruded Cretaceous strata near the surface and bulged them upward so that they dip away from the center. Since the time of that magmatic intrusion, about forty-seven million years ago, erosion has stripped off the strata which lay over the igneous rock mass called a pluton; the igneous rock of the pluton now lies bared in the center of the blister, exposed by the relentless erosion which ceaselessly attacks all mountains, large and small (Fig. 23).

The Franklin Mountains are a long, linear, north-trending range. The crustal block which includes the mountain range is bounded on the east and west by north-trending faults; this block is, therefore, called a fault block. Because the strata have been tilted from their originally horizontal position, the block is called a tilted fault block (Fig. 24). The intersection of the fault and the surface of the earth is called the trace of the fault (Fig. 25). El Paso lies in a part of the western United States which geologists refer to as the Basin and Range Province. Southern New Mexico, southern Arizona, all of Nevada, western Utah, as well as west Texas, lie in this province. It is characterized by alternating basins, like the Hueco Bolson east of the Franklin Mountains, and ranges, like the Franklin Mountains (Fig. 26). A traveler who journeys from El Paso westward to Phoenix, for example, crosses numerous basins and ranges. The type of range most characteristic of this province is the tilted fault block range. Indeed, the Franklin Mountains are perhaps one of the best developed examples of the type. Other local examples include the San Andres Mountains northeast of Las Cruces, the east Potrillo Mountains, and the Florida Mountains, south of Deming.

On the west side of South Franklin Mountain (with the white Federal Aviation Administration building on it, east of Coronado) is an erosional feature locally referred to as the Thunderbird (Fig. 27). This has been formed as the result of erosion of the gray El Paso Limestone so deeply that the underlying red rhyolite of the Thunderbird Group has been exposed so that it resembles a large bird.

Fig. 21. This view of the Southern Franklin Mountains is from the Chamizal National Memorial. Scenic Drive extends around the south end of the range, cutting through the dark ridge formed on the Upham Formation (with two TV towers on it). The letter "J" lies on the Scenic Drive Formation of the El Paso Limestone. The letter "A" (viewed edgewise and difficult to identify but visible as a white mark on the dark slopes behind a wooden telephone pole) lies on the contact of the Bliss Sandstone and the underlying Red Bluff granite. KTSM-TV tower is on the Scenic Drive Formation. The peak in the distance, seen at the far right of the photo, is South Franklin Mountain. The Chamizal National Memorial is built on the flood plain of the Rio Grande.

Fig. 22. This view of Cerro de Cristo Rey, looking toward the west from Buckley Drive, shows the prominent central core of igneous rock; however, the broad surrounding apron of slightly dipping Cretaceous strata do not show well from this distance. (Compare Fig. 23.) The broad surface in the distance is the La Mesa plain formed on the old flood plain deposits of the ancient Rio Grande.

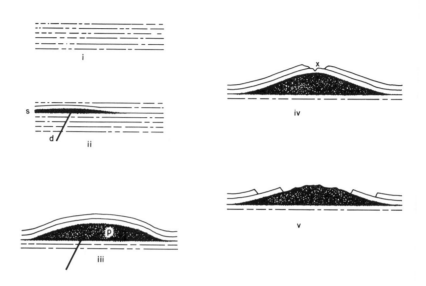

Fig. 23. This cross section diagram illustrates the development of Cerro de Cristo Rey. (i) Horizontal Cretaceous shallow water marine strata were deposited in this region about 100 million years ago. (ii) Magma was intruded into the horizontal strata along a dike (d) which injected magma beneath strata to form a broad horizontal sheet of magma called a sill (s). This occurred about 47 million years ago.
(iii) Continued magmatic pressure raised the overlying strata, probably about 1,000 feet thick, into a broad arch over one mile across. It took hundreds to thousands of years to freeze the magma to form a mass of igneous rock called a pluton. A pluton with a flat bottom and a rounded top like this is called a laccolith. (iv) Erosion began to destroy the strata which formed the roof. This began shortly after intrusion. (v) In the ensuing 47 million years erosion has deroofed the laccolith so that the igneous rock now forms the central part of Cristo Rey and the Cretaceous marine strata form a ring around the central core of the pluton.

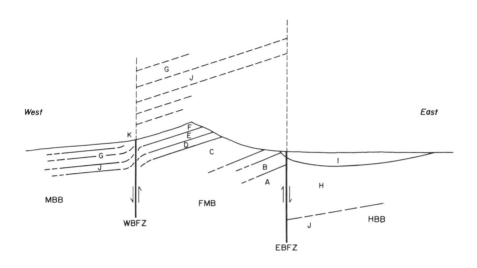

Fig. 24. The Franklin Mountains tilted fault block is shown here north of Ranger Peak. The Franklin Mountains block (FMB) has been raised with respect to the Hueco Bolson block (HBB) and the Mesilla Bolson block (MBB) along the western boundary fault zone (WBFZ) and eastern boundary fault zone (EBFZ). The oldest rocks in the range include the Castner Marble (A) and Lanoria Quartzite (B), overlain by the Thunderbird Group (C). In sequence, there are the Bliss Sandstone (D), El Paso Limestone (E), and Montoya Dolomite (F). The Hueco Limestone (J), as well as older Paleozoic beds between it and the Montoya Dolomite which used to be on the range, have been eroded away, as have been the Cretaceous strata (G). These are both preserved in the Mesilla Bolson block. Although there are no known Cretaceous strata in the Hueco Bolson block, a great thickness of much younger strata, similar to or the same as the Fort Hancock Formation (H), is in the Hueco Bolson block. (I) represents the old river deposits from which El Paso gets much of its water. The trace of the western boundary fault zone (K) at the surface is clearly visible along the western side of the range (Fig. 25).

Fig. 25. This view of the trace of the western boundary fault of the Southern Franklin Mountains is toward the east from Mesa Hills Road. The west-dipping Montoya Dolomite is shown, including the bright-colored Cutter Formation which forms the prominent peaks. Mount Franklin is at the right edge of the photo. The dark band of vegetation (white arrow) along the lower part of the mountain follows the trace of the boundary fault. The vegetation, including mesquite, yucca, creosote bush, and numerous grasses, thrives on the broken rock of the fault zone where rainwater percolates downward. The fault trace can be easily seen from Mesa Street.

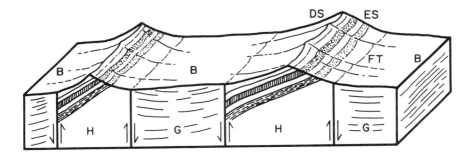

Fig. 26. This is typical basin and range structure and topography. The uplifted or range blocks, often referred to as horsts (H), are separated from the depressed or basin blocks, often referred to as grabens (G), by high angle faults. The horsts or ranges are tilted. The slope which is parallel to the inclination or dip of the beds (toward the left in the sketch) is the dip slope DS; the slope which cuts across the bedding is the erosion slope ES. Drainage from the mountains into the bolsons (B) fills them with sediment, in many places one to two miles deep. This type of structure is frequently referred to as horst and graben structure or basin and range structure and is characteristic of the Basin and Range province. The fault trace (FT), not everywhere visible, is usually covered by erosional debris or alluvium from the mountain block.

Fig. 27. This view toward the east from Cloudview Park shows the west side of South Franklin Mountain, elevation about 6,800 feet, on which are located several white buildings of the Federal Aviation Agency radio facility. Below the peak is a dark red area which resembles the outline of a thunderbird, wings outstretched, its head turned toward our left. The high light-colored peaks are formed on the Fusselman Formation of Silurian age and on the El Paso Limestone. The dark red thunderbird is formed on the Thunderbird Group of Precambrian age.

Earthquakes

Earthquakes are vibrations in the crust of the Earth caused by the movement of blocks of the crust along faults. The crust of the Earth is not stationary; it moves either up or down, to or fro, generally very slowly, but occasionally so rapidly that it produces vibrations in the rock so powerful that cracks form in the surface of the ground, parts of mountains break loose to form landslides, and poorly constructed buildings collapse. Earthquakes occur over much of the surface of the earth, but they are far more common in certain regions than in others. Earthquakes are relatively common in the Basin and Range province; historic records show no major earthquakes in the El Paso region since Don Juan de Oñate's trip in 1598, but geologic evidence indicates that major earthquakes have occurred here in the past few hundred thousand years. For example, in 1887 El Pasoans were shaken by an earthquake centered near Pueblo de Bavispe, west of El Paso in northern Mexico. Although a number of fatalities occurred near the epicenter of the earthquake, only moderate damage was recorded in the El Paso area.

The Franklin Mountains block has been rising and the Hueco Bolson block has been sinking for tens of millions of years. As each of these blocks slips past the other vertically, slowly but relentlessly, friction between them causes then to "stick" together briefly, but when they finally "slip" loose in their long-continuing slide past each other, earthquakes result. Earthquakes are associated with mountain building of the basin and are the result of this "stick-slip" process (Fig. 28).

Our present ability to predict earthquakes is very limited. Geologic evidence along the faults on either side of the Franklin Mountains suggests that the probability of significant, damaging, or catastrophic earthquakes in the El Paso region in the next hundred years is slight.

In the past few decades, minor earthquakes have been reported in the region south of El Paso International Airport. These are numerous, but they have produced no significant damage nor are they viewed as warnings of greater earthquakes to come. Neither are the few minor earthquakes reported from the eastern side of the Hueco Bolson regarded as warnings of major earthquakes. Nonetheless, the Franklin Mountains are still rising and the Hueco Bolson is still sinking. Earthquake activity is possible for hundreds of thousands of years to come.

Fig. 28. This view of North Franklin Mountain from Northeast El Paso shows the highest peak, elevation 7,198 feet, in the Franklin Mountains, formed on Precambrian Thunderbird rocks. The light cliffs are made of west-dipping Precambrian Lanoria Quartzite (see Fig. 12 for a closer view). Precambrian rocks exposed here are higher than they are elsewhere in Texas, so this is called the highest structural point in Texas. The highest topographic point in Texas is Guadalupe Peak, which is formed on Permian Limestone. At Guadalupe Peak the top of the Precambrian rocks is below sea level, much lower than it is in the Franklin Mountains where the crust of the earth has been raised structurally higher than elsewhere in Texas. The constant rising of the mountain block along faults for millions of years has been accompanied by thousands of sharp, sudden fault movements which produce earthquakes. The range is still slowly rising, and earthquakes will continue, although the rate of uplift and earthquake activity seem to be declining.

Landslides

Wherever mountain ranges exist, landslides occur during the process of erosion. In the Franklin Mountains, landsliding has occurred widely and has been extremely important in eroding the range. Were it not for this important process, the Franklin Mountains would probably be ten thousand feet higher because the strata which remain in the range are only part of the sequence that used to be part of the mountain block. Thus, as the range has been raised, it also has been eroded; as the basins have sunk, they also have been filled by the erosional debris. The Hueco and Mesilla basins have been filled with debris from the Franklin Mountains as well as with river and lake sediments from the ancestral Rio Grande and Lake Cabeza de Vaca.

Around the lower slopes and flanks of the Franklin Mountains are numerous old landslide deposits. In the city limits, the most important are Crazy Cat Mountain, McMillan Quarry, and Sugar Loaf Mountain.

Crazy Cat Mountain consists of Montoya Dolomite and Fusselman Limestone which slid off the westward-dipping El Paso Limestone more than one million years ago. The landslide probably occurred in a few minutes, as do all similar slides. Today a small remnant of the Montoya Dolomite sits high on the western flank of the Franklin Mountains in Comanche Peak (Fig. 29), a piece of the mountain that did not slide. McMillan Quarry (now Jobe Cement Products) is in a large mass of rock that slid down the east side of the range probably before the Crazy Cat slide occurred.

Fig. 29. Two views show Comanche Peak, elevation about 5,220 feet, which lies along the ridge of the Southern Franklin Mountains. It is formed of massive, dark gray, west-dipping Upham Formation. The Upham Formation overlies the thin-bedded, buff-colored Florida Mountains Formation which shows as a light band beneath the Upham Formation (photo A). The road cuts have been excavated from the Scenic Drive Formation of the El Paso Limestone. All the strata dip west about 35° (photo B). The main mass of the Upham Formation on Comanche Peak sits at a precarious angle, seemingly ready to slide off, the way snow might slide from a steeply tilted roof.

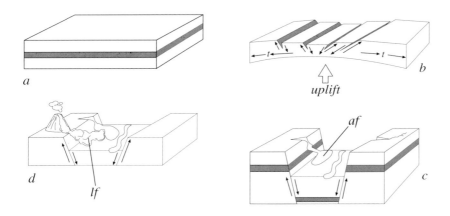

Fig. 30. These drawings show the development of a graben. (a) is a block diagram of the crust before deformation. At (b) uplift along the future graben axis produces tension (t) in the crust and normal faults develop, outlining the down-dropped graben structure. At (c) the graben has developed with a river flowing on the graben floor and tributary streams building alluvial fans (af). A volcano on the graben flank (d) adds lava flow (lf) to the graben floor.

Rio Grande Rift

From its headwaters in Colorado, the Rio Grande flows generally southerly (Fig. 2) to El Paso and then swings southeasterly. The river valley, north of El Paso, is a large graben (Fig. 2) known as the Rio Grande Rift. It is an intercontinental rift, similar to the East African Rift, the Rhine Graben of Europe, and the Lake Baikal Rift of southeastern Siberia. Intercontinental rifts form where the Earth's crust is splitting apart as a result of lateral spreading of crustal plates (Fig. 30). Our knowledge of the Rio Grande Rift is, as yet, incomplete in many details. In general, geologists presently think that the rift began to form in Eocene or Oligocene time (Table 1). Initially, an elongate arch developed over a rising mantle plume, stretching the crust on the flanks of the arch. Crustal failure occurred, and the central portion of the arch collapsed inward, forming the graben, along normal faults. As the graben or rift valley subsided, volcanoes began erupting within the rift and along its margins, pouring great volumes of volcanic lavas and volcano-derived sediment onto the valley floor. One of the easiest places to see these materials is in Selden Canyon north of Las Cruces, along the old highway between Radium Springs and Hatch. The Sierra de las Uvas and the Doña Ana Mountains near Las Cruces were two of the many active volcanoes during this stage in rift history. By late Miocene time (Table 1), most of the volcanoes had ceased to erupt, but the rift continued to subside, forming a natural channel for the ancestral Rio Grande. River sediments and lake deposits in Lake Cabeza de Vaca accumulated on top of the volcanic rocks, filling the valley, until about one million years ago when the through-flowing drainage of the Rio Grande was established. At about this time, basalt lavas were erupted from a series of volcanoes along the rift from the El Paso area to Albuquerque. The Potrillo volcanic field (pp. 7) formed in this terminal rift event.

Geologic History

This brief explanation of some of the more interesting aspects of the local geology can now be summarized in a short geologic history.

Nothing is known of the local geology from the beginning of Earth's history until about one billion years ago when marine calcareous deposits were formed by algae (Castner Marble). A brief period of basalt volcanism followed (Mundy Breccia). A thick sequence of near-shore marine sands was deposited (Lanoria Quartzite). About 980 million years ago, this sequence was covered by volcanic rocks of the Thunderbird Group and intruded by the Red Bluff Granite. There followed a span of about 500 million years for which no record exists, but during which erosion seems to have been dominant.

About 500 million years ago, the seas returned to this region, and the first deposit formed was a seashore sand (Bliss Formation). The seas spread over the region and until about 250 million years ago this region was either below sea level (when deposition occurred) or stood only a little above sea level (when erosion occurred). A thick sequence primarily of limestones accumulated in this region throughout Ordovician, Silurian, Devonian, Mississippian, Pennsylvanian, and Permian time. There is no evidence in this region of any sedimentary rocks deposited during the Triassic and Jurassic periods. The land level probably rose above sea level then and erosion occurred. In the Cretaceous period, the seas returned and spread over 50 percent of North America. About 100 million years ago, in mid-Cretaceous time, the continent rose again and the seashore migrated southeastward toward the present Gulf Coast.

During late Paleocene or early Eocene time (50 million years ago), mountain building began again in the El Paso region. Compressional forces in the crust initiated uplift and tilting of the Franklin Mountains; at about the same time, the Sierra de Juárez formed as a series of thrust sheets moving northwesterly from Mexico were folded and faulted (Fig. 18 a-v and b-iv-a and b-iv-b). Magmas within the crust were injected into the Cretaceous rocks, forming Cerro de Cristo Rey, the Campus Andesite, the Coronado Andesite, the Three Sisters hills in northwest El Paso, and the Vado Andesite. Radiometric age dates from the andesites in the Sierra de Juárez and the Campus Andesite indicate that these intrusions formed 45 to 50 million years ago. As the Franklin Mountains were uplifted, the Hueco basin sank.

From perhaps 20 million years ago (the date is not known), sediment filled in the basin as the ancestral Rio Grande flowed into the region. The basin gradually filled and Lake Cabeza de Vaca, which had formed in the Hueco Bolson, probably overflowed about one million years ago; the Rio Grande extended down to the Conchos River and finally flowed from the mountains to the sea. Numerous landslides from both sides of the Franklin Mountains occurred while sediment infilling of the basins took place. The river cut its present valley, about four hundred feet deep, in the past million years. Basalt volcanoes erupted on the La Mesa plain several hundred thousand years ago. Indians first appeared in this region probably about eleven thousand years ago. The first visits by Europeans occurred about four hundred years ago.

Perspective

Although man has been in the El Paso region for eleven thousand years, his written history covers only 3 percent of the total time he has occupied this region.

Earth history began 4.65 billion years ago with the formation of the earth, but in the El Paso region the rock record covers only the last one billion years. That record, too, is incomplete. A major nonconformity spanning 500 million years separates the Thunderbird Group from the overlying Bliss Sandstone; shorter periods of non-deposition and erosion, called unconformities, punctuate the Paleozoic rock sequence; no Triassic or Jurassic strata were deposited in the immediate area, and unconformities are present in the Tertiary rocks. Thus, rocks of El Paso's mountains and valleys record, perhaps, 30 percent of the last billion years, or about 6 percent of the history of the earth.

While this sounds as if we know twice as much geologic history as we do human history, the time spans of our histories are orders of magnitude different (4.65 billion years vs. 11,000 years). In fact, our geologic knowledge of past events which have shaped El Paso is far from complete. Although new information is continuously being added, it is obtained slowly, at considerable cost and effort. We know, broadly, much about El Paso's geologic past, but we do not know many of the important details of the events which have taken place.

Building Materials

Rapidly growing El Paso is enjoying a building boom. We are fortunate in having large local supplies of materials needed for construction. Clay for brick occurs in Cretaceous shales around Cerro de Cristo Rey. Limestone for cement occurs in Cretaceous marine beds in the Sierra de Juárez and northeast of Cerro de Cristo Rey. Sand and gravel for mortar and concrete occur in the Pliocene and Pleistocene Fort Hancock and Camp Rice formations in the basins. Crushed rock for concrete coarse aggregate and broken rock for our ubiquitous rock walls occurs in the Paleozoic and Precambrian limestones, dolomites, quartzites, and sandstones of the Franklin Mountains and Hueco Mountains. We are only two hundred miles from sources of petroleum products which give the energy needed to make brick from clay, cement from limestone, crushed rock from bedded deposits, and to dig all of these materials from the Earth. The petroleum materials, which come from the rocks of the Earth's crust, also supply us with asphalt cement for paving material and for roofing. Finally, the water without which we could not live in this desert is obtained from old river deposits of the Fort Hancock Formation on both sides of the Franklin Mountains and from the Rio Grande itself.

Modern man, like the Indians, survives because the region in which he lives is bounteous. We are fortunate here in El Paso because Earth provides for man's use much natural wealth as well as resources for farming, ranching, construction, and human habitation.

TABLE 1

Geologic Time - Names and Dates

CENOZOIC ERA:	
Recent	0.01
Pleistocene	2.0±
Wisconsinan glacial stage	
Illinoisan glacial stage	
Kansan glacial stage	
Nebraskan glacial stage	
Pliocene	7
Miocene	23
Oligocene	36
Eocene	51
Paleocene	65
MESOZOIC ERA:	
Cretaceous	136
Jurassic	190
Triassic	225
PALEOZOIC ERA:	
Permian	290
Pennsylvanian	320
Mississippian	345
Devonian	395
Silurian	430
Ordovician	500
Cambrian	570
PRECAMBRIAN EON:	4,650

TABLE 2

Geologic Column for
Mesozoic and Cenozoic Rocks

	AGE IN MILLION YEARS	NAME
CENOZOIC ERA:		
Recent		Alluvium (unnamed)
Pleistocene	-1	Camp Rice Formation
		(unconformity)
	-1 +	Fort Hancock Formation
Pliocene		
Miocene		(unconformity)
Oligocene		
Eocene	47	Cerro de Cristo Rey and Campus Andesite intrusions
Paleocene		
MESOZOIC ERA:		(unconformity)
Cretaceous	100	Boquillas Formation
		(unconformity)
		Buda Formation
		Del Rio Formation
		Anapra Formation
		Mesilla Valley Fm.
		Muleros Formation
		Smeltertown Fm.
		Del Norte Formation
		Finlay Formation
		Lagrima Formation
		Benigno Formation
	110	Cuchillo Formation
Jurassic	190	None present near El Paso
Triassic	225	None present near El Paso
PALEOZOIC ERA:	225	(unconformity)
Permian		Hueco Limestone
	280	
Pennsylvanian		Magdalena Limestone

47

TABLE 2 (Continued)

	AGE IN MILLION YEARS	NAME
	320	
Mississippian		Helms Formation
		Rancheria Formation
		Las Cruces Formation
	350	
Devonian		Percha Shale
		Canutillo Chert
	405	
Silurian		Fusselman Formation
	450	
Ordovician		Montoya Group
		El Paso Group
		Bliss Sandstone
	500	
PRECAMBRIAN EON:		
		Major unconformity
	980	Red Bluff Granite
		Thunderbird Group
	980 +	Mundy Breccia
	1,200-1,400	Castner Marble

This is a complete listing of all of the rock units exposed in the El Paso region. In general, the most visible units are the Precambrian, Ordovician, and Silurian formations in the Franklin Mountains, the four lowest Cretaceous formations in the Sierra de Juárez, and the other Cretaceous formations at Cerro de Cristo Rey. Cenozoic formations form the materials in the bolsons. An unconformity is a buried surface of erosion; it indicates that the sedimentary rocks were uplifted and eroded and that they were then covered by younger sediments.

TABLE 3

Subdivisions or Formations of
the El Paso and Montoya Groups

MONTOYA GROUP
(also Montoya Dolomite)

Cutter Formation
Aleman Formation
Upham Formation

unconformity

EL PASO GROUP
(also El Paso Limestone)

Florida Mountains Formation
Scenic Drive Formation
McKelligon Canyon Formation
Jose Formation
Victorio Hills Formation
Cooks Formation
Sierrite Formation

Richardson, in 1909, named the El Paso Limestone and the Montoya Dolomite. Subsequent detailed studies have shown that these thick sections of rock can be subdivided. Geologists have renamed the El Paso Limestone the El Paso Group and subdivided the group into formations; the Montoya Dolomite has been similarly subdivided. The Magdalena Limestone of Pennsylvanian age and the Hueco Limestone of Permian age have also been subdivided into a number of formations.

ROAD LOG
and Further Reading

The following road log utilizes paved highways suitable for passenger cars. Time required depends upon how much one wants to learn. The trip can be covered in part or as a whole. There are descriptions of geology at stops where the observer can examine the vistas of regional geology or the outcrops of rock at his feet. Short walks which can be included do not require hiking clothes or equipment.

Other road logs for local trips have been prepared by various geological organizations. Some trips require vehicles with high clearance (pick-up trucks). If four-wheel drive is indicated as needed, believe it. Geological society publications are usually printed in limited numbers and go "out-of-print" quickly. Contact individual societies for current lists, prices, etc.

PUBLICATIONS OF THE EL PASO GEOLOGICAL SOCIETY
In Print

(Order from El Paso Geological Society, Department of Geological Sciences, University of Texas at El Paso, El Paso, TX 79968.)

1972 *The stratigraphy and structure of the Sierra de Juárez, Chihuahua, Mexico*

1975 *Exploration from the Mountains to the Basins*

1982 *Symposium on the paleoenvironmental setting and distribution of the Waulsortian Facies*

1983 *Geology and Mineral Resources of North-Central Chihuahua, Mexico*

1986 *Geology of Southcentral New Mexico*

1987 *Geology of the western Delaware Basin, West Texas and Southcentral New Mexico*

1988 *Stratigraphy, tectonics, and resources of parts of Sierra Madre Occidental Province, Mexico*

1989 *Stratigraphy Field Guide, Franklin Mountains, Texas, and New Mexico*

1990 *Geological Excursions in the El Paso Area, Vol. 1, Aden Crater and Vicinity*

1992 *Energy resources of the Chihuahua desert region*

1992 *Geology and Mineral Resources of northern Sierra Madre Occidental, Mexico*

PUBLICATIONS OF THE
WEST TEXAS GEOLOGICAL SOCIETY
Pertinent to the El Paso area

No. 77-68 *Geology of Sacramento Mountains, Otero County, NM*
No. 81-74 *Lower Cretaceous Stratigraphy and Structure, Northern Mexico*
No. 82-76 *Delaware Basin Guidebook*
No. 85-81 *Structure and tectonics of Trans-Pecos Texas*
No. 88-84 *Guadalupe Mountains revisited*

A complete list of WTGS publications may be obtained from the West Texas Geological Society, P.O. Box 1585, Midland, Texas 79702; telephone 915-683-1573.

PUBLICATIONS OF THE PERMIAN BASIN SECTION,
SOCIETY OF ECONOMIC PALEONTOLOGISTS
AND MINERALOGISTS
Pertinent to the El Paso area

No. 75-15 *Geology of Eagle Mountains*
No. 83-22 *Geology of the Sierra Diablo and southern Hueco Mountains, West Texas*
No. 88-28 *Basin to Shelf facies transitions of the Wolfcampian stratigraphy of the Orogrande Basin*
No. 89-31 *The Lower Paleozoic of West Texas and southern New Mexico*

A complete list of PBS-SEPM publications may be obtained from the Permian Basin Section, SEPM, P.O. Box 1595, Midland, Texas 79702; telephone 915-683-1573. (PBS-SEPM and WTGS share office and phone.)

PUBLICATIONS OF THE
NEW MEXICO GEOLOGICAL SOCIETY
Pertinent to the El Paso area

Guidebook 20 *The Border Region (Chihuahua and the U.S.)*, 1969
Guidebook 26 *Las Cruces Country*, 1975
Guidebook 39 *Cretaceous and Laramide Tectonic Evolution of Southwestern New Mexico*, 1988
Guidebook 42 *Geology of the Sierra Blanca, Sacramento, and Capitan Ranges, New Mexico*, 1991

A complete list of NMGS publications may be obtained from the New Mexico Geological Society, Campus Station, Socorro, New Mexico 87801; telephone 505-835-5410.

In addition, the New Mexico Bureau of Mines and Mineral Resources publishes numerous technical geological titles each year. Its publication list (forty-odd pages) is available from: NMBMMR, Socorro, New Mexico 87801; telephone 505-835-5410.

Of particular interest to El Pasoans is NMBMMR Memoir 31, *Geology of the Cerro de Cristo Rey Uplift, Chihuahua and New Mexico.*

A Road Log
of the El Paso Region
From the University of Texas at El Paso
to Scenic Drive, McKelligon Canyon,
Woodrow Bean Transmountain Drive, Franklin Mountains
State Park, and return via Interstate 10

	Mileage total
1. Mesa Street at University Avenue; go east on University.	00.0
2. Continue east on University past traffic light at Stanton Street.	
3. Five-way stop; bear right on Ange Street.	00.5
4. Ange Street intersection with Rim Road. Turn right on Rim, go 0.15 mile, turn left into Tom Lea Park, **Stop 1**.	00.6

From this point, the Sierra de Juárez lies to the southwest. The lower valley, or El Paso valley, of the Rio Grande is to the southeast; the Hueco Mountains are to the east beyond the flat Hueco Bolson; the southern end of the Franklin Mountains is to the northeast; and Crazy Cat Mountain is to the north. Some of the folds in the Cretaceous limestone of the Sierra de Juárez can easily be seen from here. The Lower Valley of the Rio Grande has been incised almost 400 feet into the Fort Hancock Formation. The buff cliffs above and below the reservoir to the northeast are part of the Fort Hancock Formation. The Hueco Mountains are formed chiefly of the Hueco Limestone of Permian age. The high peak is Cerro Alto, a Tertiary igneous intrusion. Strata visible from here (Fig. 31) in the Franklin Mountains are El Paso and Montoya Group limestones. Five red and white TV towers are visible on the crest of the range. Towers 1 (by the "E") and 2 (by the "C") are built on the Upham Formation of the Montoya Group; 3 on Comanche Peak (Fig. 29) is on the Upham Formation of the Montoya; 4, Ranger Peak, is on the Scenic Drive Formation of the El Paso

53

Fig. 31. Looking northeast from Tom Lea Park toward Rim Road, the outcrop of Fort Hancock Formation in the bluffs is identified as A with Rim Road above it. Along the mountain from the left are tower 5, the north edge of the Crazy Cat landslide, tower 4 on Ranger Peak, tower 3 on Comanche Peak, and tower 2.

Group; and 5, the northernmost, is built on the Aleman Formation. Crazy Cat Mountain is a landslide mass that slipped off the western flank of the Franklins. Its northern edge is marked by the steep Upham cliff between towers 4 and 5 (Fig. 31). The southern edge of the slide probably was between towers 1 and 2. Comanche Peak is part of the Montoya group that did not slide; its position seems precarious. The Crazy Cat slide lies across the Western Boundary Fault of the Franklins but slide material has not been faulted appreciably; hence, the slide must be younger than the major faulting in this part of the range.

5. Return to Ange Street and continue on Rim Road.   00.9
6. Monument; entrance to Scenic Drive.   01.4
7. Rocks to the left are Upham Formation.   01.8
8. **Stop 2**. Scenic Drive Park; park on the right. From   01.9
   this point, the Sierra de Juárez is to the southwest
   across the Rio Grande beyond downtown El Paso
   and Juárez. Mountains in the distance to the south

in Mexico contain folded Cretaceous limestones similar to those of the Sierra de Juárez; Rio Grande Valley is to the southeast; to the east is the Hueco Bolson with the Hueco Mountains on the skyline beyond. Outcrops behind the park monument are marine limestones of the Ordovician El Paso Group to the right and Montoya Group to the left (see Figs. 15 and 16). Their depositional contact is at the base of the dark gray, mottled limestone (Upham Formation) to the left. These units were deposited about 500 million years ago in tropical, very shallow sea water supporting abundant carbonate-secreting organisms such as algae.

9. Continue east (down) on Scenic Drive. El Paso Group limestones crop out on the left.

10. El Paso Police Academy. Limestone was formerly quarried here. Just past the entrance to the academy, the depositional contact between the El Paso limestones and the underlying Bliss Sandstone is exposed. The Bliss, a rusty red/brown, well-bedded unit, was deposited as a beach sand during the early part of the Ordovician Period.   02.5

11. Gravelly clay of the Fort Hancock Formation overlaps the Bliss along the left side of the road. The Fort Hancock has been raised about 400 feet above the Hueco Bolson by fault displacement on the Eastern Boundary Fault.   02.8

12. Intersection of Scenic Drive and Wheeling; bear left. Scenic Drive becomes Richmond Avenue here.   02.9

13. Traffic light at Richmond and Alabama; turn left on Alabama and drive north. On the left, a fault scarp shows the location of at least one part of the Eastern Boundary Fault. Another part of the fault is further east, probably under the Patriot Freeway.   03.3

14. Traffic light at Alabama and Nashville. Continue on Alabama.   03.7

15. Traffic light at Alabama and Fort Boulevard; continue on Alabama.   04.1

16. Intersection of Alabama and McKinley. The parking lot for the KTSM-TV tramway, which is no longer open to the public, is quarried out of Red Bluff Granite 980 million years old. A short dis- 04.3

tance up the hill, the Bliss Sandstone lies on the Red Bluff. A cream-colored band of rock in the Bliss is a felsite sill radiometrically dated at 28 million years. To the north is McKelligon Canyon, formed along a fault which has dropped Sugar Loaf Mountain, on the right, several thousand feet down with respect to the main range on the left. The mountain being quarried by Jobe Concrete Products, Inc., is a landslide block which slid off the range from the great amphitheater-like hollow below the highest TV tower on the ridge to the north. To the east are the Hueco Mountains and Hueco Bolson. The high peak in the Hueco Mountains is Cerro Alto, an intrusive rock (a type called syenite) probably about the same age as Cristo Rey and the Campus Andesite (about 47 million years old). From the tramway observation tower built on the Scenic Drive Formation of the El Paso Group, one can see over 100 miles in almost all directions. Directly to the north is the continuation of the Franklin Mountains. To the northeast are the Sacramento Mountains with Sierra Blanca at their north end. Sierra Blanca is an early Cenozoic intrusive (like Cerro Alto and Cristo Rey); its north side contained the southernmost Pleistocene glacier in the United States. The western boundary of the Sacramento Mountains is also the eastern edge of the Basin and Range Province. The bolson on the west side of the Sacramento Mountains is separate from the one between the Franklin and Hueco Mountains. It is called the Tularosa Bolson; White Sands National Monument and Lake Lucero are both in the Tularosa Bolson. To the southeast, one can see the Quitman Mountains, the southeast border of the Hueco Bolson. The Rio Grande leaves the Hueco Bolson at the south side of the Quitman Mountains. To the south, one can see the great sand dune field near Samalayuca, Chihuahua, Mexico, and many mountain ranges extending far south into the Mexican section of the Basin and Range Province. To the southwest is the Sierra de Juárez in which folded Cretaceous strata can readily be seen. Cerro de Cristo Rey lies to the west and the Campus Hills lie in line with the Sierra de Juárez on the near side of the Rio Grande. Both of these groups of hills are formed on andesite, about 47 million years old. On the west side of the Franklin Mountains to the southwest is Crazy Cat Mountain, a great mass of Montoya and Fusselman formations which was originally on the Franklin Mountains. A section of strata over 600 feet thick, 1.5 miles long, and 0.9 mile wide, slipped along the base of the Montoya and crashed out onto the surface next to the range. The northern edge of the slide broke away from the vertical cliff of dark gray Upham Formation 1,000 feet north of the observation tower. The rocks which lie beneath the tramway belong to the following formations: TOP - Scenic Drive Formation: light gray, well-bedded limestone. McKelligon Canyon Formation: light gray, well-bedded limestone. Jose Formation: dark gray, massive limestone. Victorio Hills Formation: light gray, well-bedded limestone. Cooks and Sierrite Formations: tan, well-bedded limestone. Bliss Sandstone: dark red to brownish red, well-bedded limestone. Felsite sill: cream-colored light rock in the Bliss Sandstone (radiometric age 28 million years, probably older). More Bliss Sandstone. BOTTOM - Red Bluff Granite. Return to Alabama Street and turn left.

17. Quarry in El Paso Group limestones on left. White band on mountainside above quarry is the felsite sill which was emplaced between sedimentary rock beds at least 28 million years ago; however, its radiometric age is thought to be erroneously low.   04.6

18. Traffic light at Alabama and McKelligon Canyon Road. Turn left for trip into McKelligon Canyon. William Beaumont Army Medical Center is now directly behind you.   05.2

19. Intersection with five-way stop; continue straight ahead. Sugar Loaf Peak, immediately to the right, is part of a fault block which slipped off the east face of the Franklins. McKelligon Canyon is a valley   05.3

which follows along the McKelligon Canyon Fault, along which the Sugar Loaf block slid. The Sugar Loaf block is composed of Ordovician limestones and sandstones, capped by a bit of Fusselman Dolomite (Silurian).

20. Retention dam above V.F.W. Post 812 diagonally to the right.   05.5

21. Gates. Rocks in this road cut are El Paso Paso Group limestones.   05.8

22. Rocks straight ahead and slightly left beyond the canyon appear to be folded, but they are not. The beds dip toward the main canyon floor and erosion by small tributary arroyos causes the edge of each layer to trace a pattern sloping downstream on either side of the arroyo. This produces a "V" as seen from above and the optical illusion of folds when viewed from the road.   05.9

23. Road crosses main canyon; Precambrian Red Bluff Granite on the left and Ordovician El Paso Group limestones right.   06.2

    Viva El Paso theater entrance.   06.4

    Road forks; bear left.   07.5

24. Road forks to a loop; bear right.   07.6

25. **Stop 4**. Park in entrance to small, blocked side road. Walk about 200 yards up the trail to observe the nonconformity between the 500 million-year-old Ordovician Bliss Sandstone and the 980 million-year-old Red Bluff Granite. The nonconformity is marked by an arrow painted on the rock in the arroyo. This is an old Precambrian erosion surface which was buried by the beach sands of the Bliss as the sea advanced over this area in early Ordovician time. Place your hand on this nonconformity and realize that the gap in the geologic record spans almost half a billion years. Retrace your route to Alabama Street.   07.9

26. Intersection of McKelligon Canyon Road and Alabama; turn left and remain in left lane. Alabama here is built on an alluvial fan deposited at the mouth of McKelligon Canyon. Beaumont Medical Center is also situated on the alluvial fan.   10.4

27. Intersection of Alabama and Fred Wilson Road; bear left on Alabama. Road cuts for the next two miles are in Pleistocene bolson fill deposits. Gravelly beds are old alluvial fans; finer grained, buff-colored silt and clay beds are part of the Fort Hancock Formation.　　　　11.0

28. Water tank on top of fault scarp on left.　　　　12.6

29. Trinity Presbyterian Church on left. Fault scarp behind the church is part of the Eastern Boundary Fault system of the Franklins. Alabama becomes Magnetic here. Continue north on Magnetic.　　　　13.1

30. Intersection of Magnetic and Hercules. Continue north on Magnetic.　　　　13.3

31. Magnetic and Hondo Pass. Turn right on Hondo Pass. Get into left lane as you go down Hondo Pass.　　　　14.3

32. Traffic light at Gateway South.　　　　15.1

33. Traffic light at Gateway North. Turn left. Stay on Gateway. National Guard Armory on right. Do not enter Patriot Freeway.　　　　15.2

34. Intersection with Diana Drive. Stay on Gateway. Transmountain Campus, El Paso Community College, on right.　　　　16.1

Cohen Sportsplex on right.　　　　16.3

　　　　16.7

35. Intersection of Gateway and Woodrow Bean Transmountain Drive (Loop 375). Turn left and continue west on Transmountain.　　　　17.2

36. Entrance to Wilderness Park Museum on right. Just past the entrance, a sweeping curve toward the left begins.　　　　17.8
[Note: At the stops along Transmountain Drive, be *very* careful. Traffic moves at high speed - pull well onto the shoulder to park; be careful if you venture onto the roadway. Also, *do not* climb on the outcrops. They are unstable and are very likely to collapse under or upon you!]

37. **Stop 5**. First major road cut. A spectacular display of geologic features is exposed in this cut. The rocks include Precambrian Red Bluff Granite, Castner Marble, and basalt. Numerous narrow dikes of granite and basalt cut through the host rocks. At the uphill (west) end of the cut, beds of　　　　18.6

the Castner Marble are vertical, steeply tilted by intrusion of the granite. To the east, the Hueco Bolson forms the flat valley floor. It is the major ground water reservoir which supplies El Paso's drinking water. Tom Cliett, retired El Paso Water Utilities geologist, provided the following remarks about the ground water system: "In 1978, El Paso Water Utilities produced over 10 billion gallons (92,307.6 acre feet) of water of which only a little over 1 billion gallons were taken from the Rio Grande. The rest is groundwater taken from sands and gravels of the Hueco Bolson between the Franklin Mountains and the Hueco Mountains, and from the Mesilla Bolson near Canutillo on the west side of the Franklins. "The Hueco Bolson is partly filled with lake and river deposits. The ancient Rio Grande that deposited large volumes of sand and gravel flowed on the east side of the Franklins during the Pleistocene. These deposits form the freshwater aquifer for El Paso. Wells in this aquifer supplied 69 percent of the total groundwater produced in 1978. [In 1990, El Pasoans used 35.3 billion gallons drawn from the Hueco Bolson (~65%), the Rio Grande (~20%), and the Mesilla Bolson (~15%).] "In the Hueco Bolson, over 10.5 million acre feet (one acre foot = 325,000 gallons) of fresh water are available for public use. About 5,600 acre feet per year are added to the aquifer from rainfall on the east side of the Franklins; at the present rate of withdrawal, this supply will last well into the next century. There are also at least 2 million acre feet of brackish (partly salty) water that can either be blended with fresh water or desalinated (desalted) for use." Mr. Cliett's comments will be continued at **Stop 8**. Continue to drive up (west) Transmountain Drive.

38. Precambrian granite exposed in road cut (right).   19.4
39. Second major road cut. **Stop 6**. Castner Marble   19.8
    exposed on the right. Heat from igneous activity recrystallized the limestone into marble and igneous solutions deposited a variety of minerals in the marble. Most common are reddish-brown,

twelve-sided garnet crystals. Apple-green epidote is
responsible for the green in the marble.
Sedimentary features of the original limestone,
such as conglomerates and soft-sediment folds, are
well preserved. At the west (uphill) end of this outcrop, the Mundy Basalt Breccia is exposed on the   19.9
slope beside the road. Continue westerly on
Transmountain/Loop 375.

40. Third major road cut. A small section of Lanoria   20.1
Quartzite is exposed at the east end of the cut;
however, the main rocks here are dark gray gran-
ites. Elsewhere, this granite is intruded by the Red
Bluff Granite and therefore must be somewhat
older than the Red Bluff. Here it forms a sill about
1,000 feet thick in the Lanoria Quartzite. The dominant mineral of the granite is a dark gray micro-
cline feldspar that occurs as crystals up to 1 cm
long. A diabase (very dark, very fine-grained mafic
rock) dike cuts the granite near the western end of
the cut.

41. To the left is Fusselman Canyon, formed on the   20.4
Fusselman Canyon Fault. The rocks on the far
(south) side have been dropped more than 1,000
feet. The fault itself loops back to the south and
connects with the northern end of the McKelligon
Canyon fault.

42. Road cut to the right is in the lower member of the   20.7
Lanoria Quartzite. To the left, across Fusselman
Canyon, there is a reddish "trench" extending
down the hillside. This "trench" is formed along
an outcrop of the diabase dike (**Stop 6**) because
the diabase weathers more rapidly than the host
rocks. Continue along Transmountain Drive. Begin
working into the left lane.

43. Fourth major road cut, along the curve up to the   21.8
pass. The rocks here belong to the Thunderbird
Group, a complex of volcanic rocks and sedimentary rocks composed of volcanic debris. The rock is
faulted and is intruded by diabase dikes. Rock
slides, especially after rain or snowfall, frequently
occur along the faults. The slopes are extremely
unstable - *do not venture onto them*. The

Thunderbird Group is more than 1,000 feet thick and is the youngest Precambrian rock in the area. Deep weathering of the diabases makes them unsuitable for radiometric dating, but they are clearly much younger than the rocks they cut along Transmountain Drive.

44. Cross over to Observation Point on the west side of highway. **Stop 7**. Park and walk to barrier. OBEY WARNING SIGNS. This is a superb panoramic view of the region west of the Rio Grande's Upper Valley. Beginning in the north, one may see the Robledo Mountains (by Las Cruces); just to the west is the Sierra de las Uvas Dome; west of that is Cooke's Peak in Cooke's Range (peak is high, sharp); still further west are the Florida Mountains (the distant range beyond the closer Potrillos); the cinder cones of the Potrillo volcanic field (low, rounded hills); the three prominent peaks to the west include Mount Riley and Mount Cox (intrusive rocks like Cerro de Cristo Rey); the low ridge to the south of Mount Riley is the East Potrillo Mountains (a tilted fault block like the Franklins, but much smaller); the Sierra de Juárez to the left (SW); and Cerro de Cristo Rey (with the cross on top). Closer in, just east of I-10, the Three Sisters are small plutons of andesite in sedimentary rocks. The low hills just out from the front of the Franklins are formed of Hueco Limestone (Permian); and the Western Boundary Fault is at the foot of the slope below. Approximately 8,000 feet of movement has occurred on the fault in this part of the range. Road cuts on the north side of the highway are in the Thunderbird Group. High up on the slopes, one can see extensive deposits of boulder alluvium derived from the Thunderbird rocks of North Franklin Mountain. Carefully drive back across the highway and proceed to the west.   22.1

45. Road cuts to the right are in vertical beds of El Paso limestones.   22.9

46. Entrance to Franklin Mountains State Park (formerly called Tom Mays Park). *Take nothing but pictures and your trash from the park. Leave nothing but foot-*   24.7

prints. Optional side trip: Entrance sign. North Franklin Peak, highest on skyline, is formed of Thunderbird Group rocks. At 1 mile from the entrance, bear right on the side road. Continue on to picnic area about 2.1 miles from entrance. Park. The rocks near the picnic shelters to the west are Permian Hueco Limestone and were faulted down relative to the rest of the range in a series of faults which trend along the range front. Fusulinids (1 cm, spindle-shaped shells of single-cell animals) and a variety of other marine fossils are present in the limestones here. To the east, the low slopes are El Paso Group limestones; to the southeast, the Precambrian Thunderbird Group and Red Bluff Granite are exposed on the upper slopes. An abandoned mine high in the canyon yielded unprofitable amounts of copper and other minerals. Retrace your route back to the intersection of the park road and Transmountain Drive.

47. **Stop 8**. Parking area immediately west of Franklin Mountains State Park entrance. Discussion of Canutillo Well Field, El Paso's water supply, by Mr. Cliett: "In 1978, the Canutillo area supplied 28 percent of El Paso's water, an amount that could probably be doubled without significantly depleting the aquifer. This field is smaller than the Hueco Bolson, but is close to areas of recharge by ground water from the Mesilla Bolson to the west. This aquifer is also composed of loose sands and gravel deposited by the Rio Grande." Continue west (down) on Transmountain Drive. 24.7

48. Intersection of Transmountain and I-10; turn left (south) and enter I-10 southbound. 28.2

49. To the west, Mounts Cox and Riley rise above the La Mesa Plain. To the south (straight ahead) are the Sierra de Juárez; just to their left is Cerro de Cristo Rey; a bit more to the left the prominent hill is the northernmost of the Three Sisters; South Mount Franklin peak has the FFA towers on top; due east is North Franklin Mountain (highest peak in the range at 7,198 feet, formed of Thunderbird Group rocks); and to the northeast of it is 28.8

Anthony's Nose, a peak formed on Silurian
Fusselman Dolomite.

50. To the east (left) are three low, rounded hills called
    the Three Sisters, formed of andesite like that in
    Cerro de Cristo Rey, intruded into Cretaceous sedi-
    mentary rocks. Cristo Rey is almost straight ahead.
    The Rio Grande occupies a flood plain several
    miles wide to the west.   31.2

52. Intersection of I-10 and Mesa Street. Continue on
    the interstate. As you pass over Mesa Street, the red
    "thunderbird" (Fig. 27) formed by outcrops of the
    Thunderbird Group is clearly visible on the slopes
    of South Franklin Mountain, below the FAA tow-
    ers. Low on the slope, extending southerly, a dark
    band of heavy vegetation marks the trace of the
    Western Boundary Fault of the Franklins (Fig. 25).   32.8

53. Resler Drive overpass.   34.4

54. Exit 13, Sunland Park and Doniphan Drive.
    Continue south on I-10. About a half mile past this
    exit, the Interstate begins a gentle climb through
    road cuts in the Fort Hancock Formation, the
    ancient sediments deposited in Lake Cabeza de
    Vaca. At the top of the grade, the view changes.
    The Campus Hills, ahead and to the left, are com-
    posed of andesite; the Sierra de Juárez is directly
    ahead, across the river which here flows through
    "El Paso del Norte del Rio Bravo," or the "Pass of
    the North." The quarry to the right is in
    Cretaceous limestone. Some of these limestones
    also crop out along the flanks of Cerro de Cristo
    Rey, to the right and across the river.   35.0

55. Exit 16, Executive Center Boulevard. Stay on I-10.   38.0

56. Campus Hills andesite to the left, ASARCO smelter
    to right. Begin working to right lane.   38.8

57. Rio Grande and Mexico to right.   39.8

58. Exit 18, Schuster Avenue and UTEP. Take this exit.   40.1

59. Turn left under overpass.   40.3

60. Turn left at traffic light at Sunbowl Drive.   40.4

61. Turn right on University Avenue to starting point.   40.5

Acknowledgments

This book was written at the request of the El Paso Geological Society. Numerous attempts in the past to present an introductory explanation of the geology of the El Paso region have met with various difficulties. The present book represents the culmination of efforts spread over a period of years, an answer to inquiries received by members of the Society for information on the subject.

Many people have helped in this endeavor. Ms. Angela Sanchez typed the manuscript and assisted editorially. Clay Martin prepared the sketches ofCerro de Cristo Rey andredrafted several of the author's sketches in the text. Profesor William Strain helped in preparing the road log which is presented at the end of the book. Mr. Thomas Cliett, ground water geologist for the El Paso Public Service Board, prepared the section on the ground water of the El Paso region. The El Paso Geological Society officers, who allowed the author the freedom to prepare the book, receive my sincerest thanks. Finally, the Editor of Texas Western Press, Dr. Haywood Antone, has been most helpful in meeting the deadline and aidng the author in the final stages of presentation of the manuscript. To all I offer my sincerest appreciation. I hope that all the effort was worth it.

Earl M. P. Lovejoy
Department of Geological Sciences
The University of Texas at El Paso
February 1980